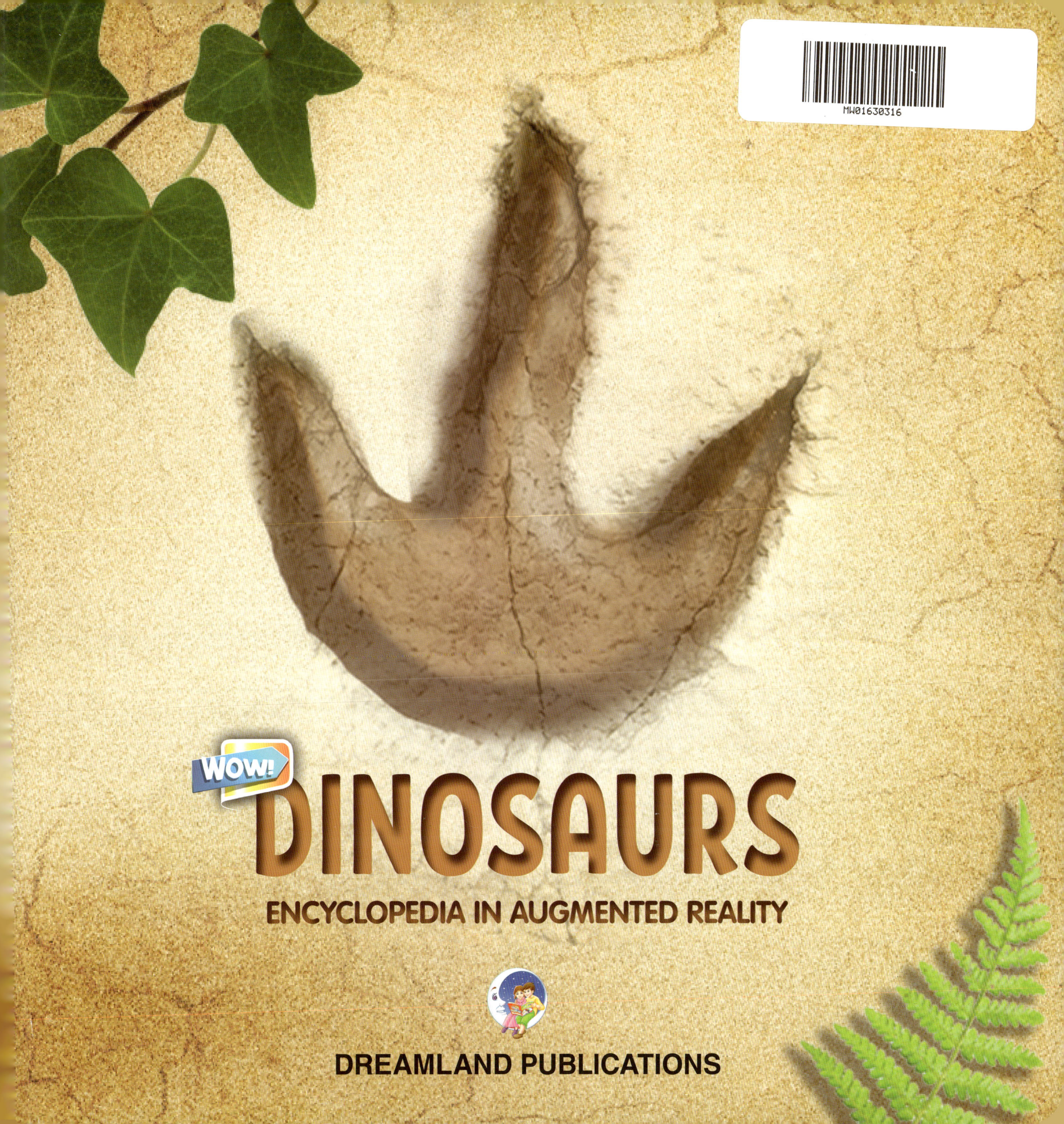

WOW!
DINOSAURS
ENCYCLOPEDIA IN AUGMENTED REALITY
DREAMLAND PUBLICATIONS

CONTENTS

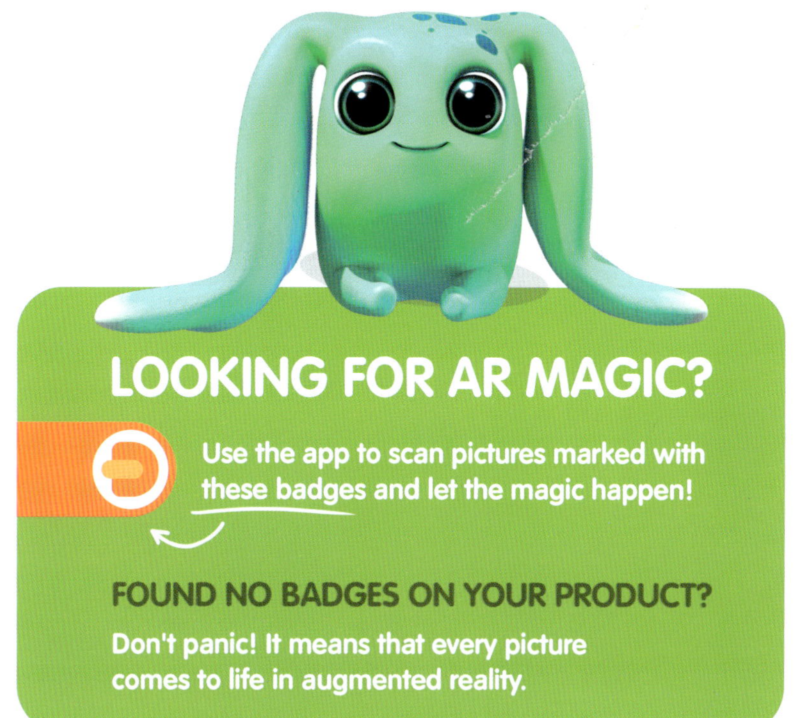

If you have any questions, please email us at
help@devar.org
We are always ready to help!
More about us: www.devar.org

devar_official

Dear friend,

Are you ready for a tour full of mysteries, wonders, and incredible adventures? How would you like to become the main character of your own story? Are you ready to change the world? Now you can do all this and more because this is not an ordinary book at all . . .

Inspired by the discoveries of great travellers and inventors, DEVAR has explored the strangest and most unusual phenomena not only in our universe but beyond it. We have created a whole world where absolutely anything is possible! It is broader than our reality. Time and space, rules and regulations, limits and conventions have no hold on it. This world is waiting for you, our daring reader, and you are the one who can give it life!

You can conquer the most dangerous and mysterious places on our planet, go to space, and even travel through time! What else? Whatever you want! You will make wonderful discoveries, do bold experiments, meet great people and unbelievable creatures. Change this world the way you want to!

This isn't magic or alien technology. This is augmented reality! A special technology that helps add to the world around you.

Face it, you can't wait to try, can you?

Welcome to the world of DEVAR!

DEAR FUTURE EXPLORERS

ANNIE

DANNY

FILL IN YOUR NAME

HI, ...! MY NAME IS ANNIE, AND THIS IS MY BROTHER DANNY. TOGETHER WE EXPLORE THE MANY WONDERS AND MYSTERIES OF THE WORLD. THOUGH MORE OFTEN THAN NOT WE GET INTO A MESS. ONCE WE MET A REAL LION, CAN YOU BELIEVE THAT? HAPPILY, OUR KNOWLEDGE AND QUICK WIT ALWAYS HELP US TO FIND A WAY OUT!

I'VE HEARD YOU LIKE DINOSAURS. I ABSOLUTELY ADORE THEM! BY THE WAY, WE ARE GOING ON AN EXPEDITION TO THE MESOZOIC ERA – THIS IS THE TIME WHEN DINOSAURS WALKED THE EARTH. DO YOU WANT TO JOIN US? IT'S GOING TO BE GREAT! THERE ARE SO MANY INTERESTING THINGS WE CAN SHOW YOU! BUT FIRST WE NEED TO GET READY. YOU CAN'T SET OFF FOR ADVENTURES WITHOUT KNOWLEDGE.

PALAEONTOLOGY is scientific study of ancient extinct animals and plants. The term was coined by Henri Marie Ducrotay de Blainville in 1822. This doesn't mean people didn't study palaeontology before then, but the science didn't yet have a name.

PALAEONTOLOGIST is a scientist who studies palaeontology. He or she carries out archaeological digs, explores geological layers, and looks for fossils of animals, plants, or insects. The deeper the fossil, the more ancient it is!

4

FOSSILS are remains or impressions of ancient organisms that are found during archaeological digs. Such discoveries play a very important role in palaeontology. They help scientists reconstruct an ancient animal or plant—providing a piece of the puzzle so palaeontologists can make conclusions about what the organism looked like and how and where it lived.

People from the ancient Roman Empire found giant fossils and used them as medicine and thought they had magical powers. The fossils were considered to be remains of ancient mythological animals, most often . . . **DRAGONS!**

Many of these beliefs continued up until 1824, when British palaeontologist William Buckland and French naturalist Georges Cuvier studied the remains of ancient bones and believed that they could be from a giant, predatory lizard. They gave this creature the name Megalosaurus, which means **GIANT LIZARD.**

This marks the beginning of the study of dinosaurs, although, the word "dinosaur" doesn't appear until 1842 when it was coined by Richard Owen. The word means "terrible lizard," which is a great name for these giant creatures that were several times larger than elephants, rhinos, and all of the known land animals of that time!

Up until the beginning of the 20th century, scientists believed all dinosaurs to be huge and slow. But in the early 1960s, John Ostrom, an ambitious student from Yale University, proposed a new theory. He believed that dinosaurs were more like huge, flightless birds than lizards. A lot of dinosaur species had hollow bones and long tails to maintain balance. This theory was revolutionary and helped develop a brand-new scientific question: What if birds originated from dinosaurs? This theory is considered generally accepted today.

There have been many discoveries during the more than 200 years of active study of dinosaurs; however, there remain many unsolved mysteries.

MAYBE YOU CAN SOLVE THEM?

THE AGE OF THE DINOSAURS

Our planet formed about 4.5 billion years ago. It has gone through many changes since then. Scientists who study the Earth's development have named several main stages in its history.

These stages are called eras, and each era is divided into periods. Each period lasts several million years.

> The Palaeozoic era or the era of "ancient life"
541-252 MILLION YEARS AGO

> The Mesozoic era or the era of "middle life"
252-66 MILLION YEARS AGO

> The Cenozoic era or the era of "new life"
66 MILLION YEARS AGO-NOW

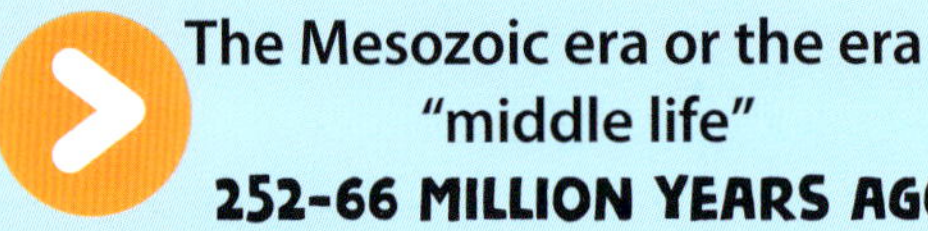

The Palaeozoic era gave birth to life on Earth. Many invertebrates inhabited Earth's water—especially its warm seas. The only life on land were the first plants.

Some fish species evolved to the point of being able to live on land. They could breathe with primitive lungs.

Millions of years passed until some of these creatures evolved into someone larger and more dangerous—dinosaurs!

Dinosaurs appeared on the planet during the Mesozoic Era and dominated until the end of the era. The dinosaurs differed greatly: they were large and small, carnivore and herbivore. The word "dinosaur" is often used for all ancient lizards, but this is not quite right. All ancient reptiles had one ancestor—the archosaur. *Dinosaurus* is a group of reptiles that lived **ON LAND** only. All the rest have other names. For instance, flying reptiles are called pterosaurs and swimming reptiles are called plesiosaurs. You will learn a lot about these unusual creatures in this book.

The Mesozoic Era is divided into three periods: the Triassic, the Jurassic and the Cretaceous. At the end of the Jurassic period, the supercontinent Pangaea split into Gondwana and Laurasia. They were separated by a large ancient ocean, Tethys. Later, Gondwana split again into two parts: western and eastern.

The movement of these continents continued into the Cenozoic era, until they took up the positions we know today.

The name **"PANGAEA"** is derived from the ancient Greek meaning **"ENTIRE LAND."** The name was coined by German geologist Alfred Lothar Wegener.

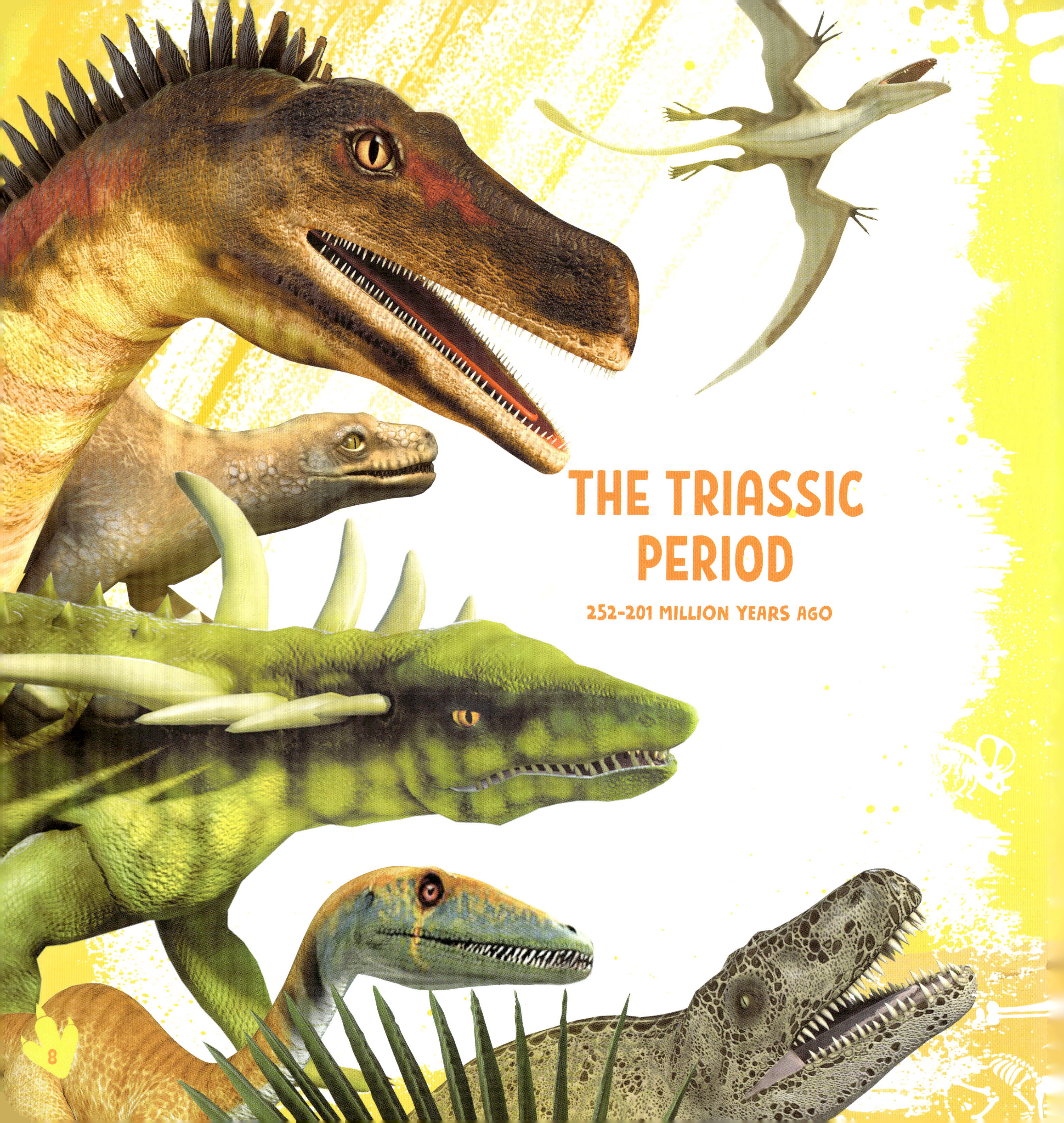
THE TRIASSIC PERIOD
252-201 MILLION YEARS AGO
8

The Triassic period was a very uneasy time and such events were quite common. Although the first dinosaurs were just evolving, the world around tested them in full because the supercontinent Pangaea was splitting into two parts. This caused constant earthquakes and eruptions that resulted in drought and other disasters. But dinosaurs survived and managed to adapt.

The climate was hot. Almost the whole land reminded a lifeless desert. Shallow seas dried out, and the deeper ones became unbearably salty.

CLIMATE

FAUNA

Carnivorous reptiles called archosaurs (ancestors of today's crocodiles) dominated on land. Marine animals still remained the largest and most dangerous predators on the planet. The first insects and spiders appeared during this time.

FLORA

There was no grass or flowers. Only hardy plants such as snake grass and a few types of ginkgo could bear the harsh conditions. Giant ferns sometimes flourished during rare rainy periods.

ARIZONASAURUS

243–200 MILLION YEARS AGO

Carnivore

TRIASSIC PERIOD

We know little about the arizonasaurus as scientists have found only two remaining fossil samples! The first discovery was made by American palaeontologist Samuel Paul Welles in 1947. He found a jaw and several teeth in the Moenkopi Formation (Arizona, USA).

Fifty years later, another American palaeontologist, Sterling Nesbitt, found an almost complete skeleton.

DINO FACTS

Diet:
Water and land animals

Meaning of the name:
"Arizona lizard"

According to modern explorations, arizonasauruses were not actually dinosaurs. They belong to archosaurs, the ancient reptiles that inhabited the planet during the Triassic period. They were a dominating species and the top of the food chain before dinosaurs reigned.

Its back was decorated with a hump, which scientists call a sail. It was formed by spines growing from the vertebrae. This made the body agile but limited the arizonasaurus's ability to turn its head.

Nobody knows for sure, why arizonasaurus needed its sail.

Some scientists believe this lizard was cold-blooded, so it used its sail for temperature control. The sail helped save and distribute warmth during sunbathing. However, it could also be cooled quickly by moving to the shade when the lizard felt too hot.

There is also a belief that the sail could function much like a camel's hump. That means the arizonasaurus stored fat and nutritious substances to maintain energy in times of food shortages.

Some scientists believe that only males had sails in order to attract females, much like peacocks with their beautiful tails.

One more theory is that the sail produced scary sounds while the animal moved in order to frighten enemies.

BATRACHOTOMUS
242-237 MILLION YEARS AGO

Carnivore

TRIASSIC PERIOD

Where was it found?
Swabia, Germany

Batrachotomuses looked like crocodiles, so scientists believe they also lived near bodies of water such as moors, which were plentiful during the Triassic period.

Like crocodiles, the batrachotomus was covered with bony plates. These plates were probably not joined in one shell—they were attached to each other by muscles. Such bony shell made this reptile fast and agile during the hunt and while attacking prey.

DINO FACTS

Diet:
fish, ancient amphibians
Meaning of the name:
"frog cutting"

Even though its name means "frog cutting" some scientists believe its teeth were not strong enough to prey on large amphibians. It could probably only eat fish.

12

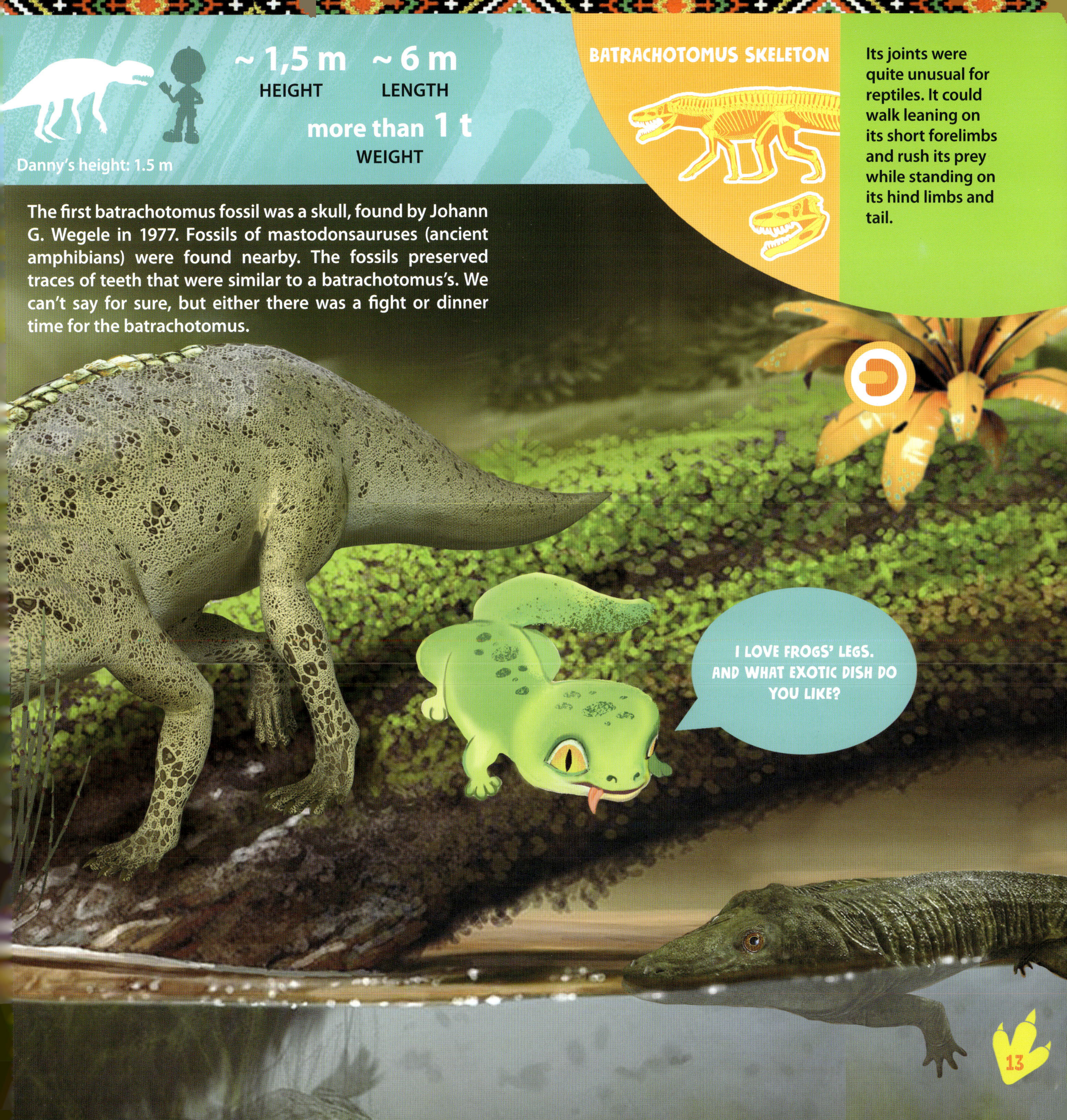

The first batrachotomus fossil was a skull, found by Johann G. Wegele in 1977. Fossils of mastodonsauruses (ancient amphibians) were found nearby. The fossils preserved traces of teeth that were similar to a batrachotomus's. We can't say for sure, but either there was a fight or dinner time for the batrachotomus.

DESMATOSUCHUS 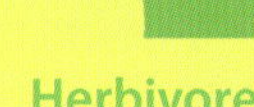

230-200 MILLION YEARS AGO

Herbivore

TRIASSIC PERIOD

The desmatosuchus lived in the moorlands of the North America and was probably a herbivore due to the shape and state of the teeth, which didn't have notches or serrated edges. Scientists believe it ate soft plant material, like ferns.

The desmatosuchus's whole body was covered with bony plates along with two rows of spines that ran along its back. The longest spines were near the forelimbs. This gave the desmatosuchus protection from predators.

Despite similarities, it was not a crocodile. It was not even a dinosaur. It was a member of the archosaur group. That was the group from which dinosaurs and many other species evolved.

DESMATOSUCHUS SKELETON

It had a long beaky snout, a short neck, an elongated body, and a long tail. The shape of its snout was sort of like a shovel. The limbs were quite short, with forelimbs much shorter than hind limbs.

Desmatosuchuses were abundant in the late Triassic period. Their remains are often found together with other reptiles that lived near bodies of water. Relying on this fact, scientists suppose they also lived near rivers and lakes.

Moreover, desmatosuchus skeletons are often found together. This could mean they lived in groups or families.

Some scientists see several similarities with armadillos. Both groups have long snouts that lack teeth on the end; their shells also have much in common. As armadillos prey on insects, scientists suppose that the desmatosuchus could have done the same.

15

PLATEOSAURUS

220-210 MILLION YEARS AGO

Herbivore

TRIASSIC PERIOD

Herds of plateosauruses were scattered along the lowlands and forests of Europe during the late Triassic period. As they ate their way through the forests, they created pathways that kept them safe from predators.

Fossil examination shows that plateosaurus teeth were not adapted for chewing. Most likely they swallowed stones to help them grind and digest their leafy diet.

By the way, such stones are called gastroliths. Some living animals do this to grind food in the stomach. But that's not a good idea for humans.

Each forelimb had five fingers. They were good for grasping leaves. And its claws could be used to cut branches.

Its hind limbs were well developed. Scientists believe that these dinosaurs were excellent runners. They used their agile tail to balance when turning. To save themselves from predators they could run up to 40 km/h. That is faster than the fastest Olympic runner in the world!

It had an elongated skull with eyes on the sides. That helped the plateosaurus always be alert. Plateosaurus walked on its toes, which were grouped together. That made the dinosaur stable on the moorlands. Sometimes these are called elephant's feet.

Scientists have found a lot of plateosaurus fossils. They thoroughly examined them and found out that plateosauruses became adults at about twelve years old and lived to around the age of twenty. The youngest skeleton found was ten, the oldest, twenty-seven. That's about the lifespan of cows, for example.

EUDIMORPHODON

210-200 MILLION YEARS AGO

TRIASSIC PERIOD

The eudimorphodon was not a dinosaur. It was a pterosaur or flying reptile.

During the late Triassic period, eudimorphodons were flying along the shores of western Europe. They were supposedly able to plunge like an arrow in the water, just like gannets do today. This hunting method requires good eyesight to see the prey under the water's surface and strong muscles to rise back into the air.

The first fossils were found in 1973 by Mario Pandolfi in the town of Cene, Italy. Palaeontologist Rocco Zambelli described them and came up with idea that they could fly. He also believed that their diet was fish as some of the fossils he studied showed fish remains in the area of the stomach.

Eudimorphodons had the teeth of a predator: sharp front fangs to catch its prey and multi-pointed back teeth to chew it. Pterosaurs had 110 teeth in a jaw that was only 6 centimetres long!

Scientists still have an unsolved mystery: How did the eudimorphodon fly with such a flexible tail? Other long-tailed pterosaurs had stiff, immobile vertebral extensions to balance for flight, but the tail of eudimorphodon ended with a kite-like flap. The role of this remains unknown.

The wings were well developed. This is evident from the bone structure of the forelimbs. The wings were probably bat-like with a skin membrane between the limbs and body. This helped manoeuvring in the air.

COELOPHYSIS

215-200 MILLION YEARS AGO

Carnivore

TRIASSIC PERIOD

These sly predators inhabited the forests of the late Triassic period and preyed near bodies of water. They probably hunted in groups so they could attack large dinosaurs.

Scientists compared the eye structures of the coelophysis, birds, and reptiles. They discovered that the coelophysis's keen eyesight could make it able to prey day and night. Their eyesight was superior to that of most reptiles and was most similar to living birds of prey such as eagles and hawks.

DINO FACTS

Diet:
fish, reptiles, other dinosaurs

Meaning of the name:
"hollow form"

A coelophysis skull went to space! On January 22, 1998, the shuttle Endeavor brought it to the Mir space station!

1 m HEIGHT

~3 m LENGTH

up to **45 kg** WEIGHT

Danny's height: 1.5 m

Keen eyesight and an agile body made the coelophysis fast, dangerous, and bold predators. They probably developed primitive hunting strategies and are thought to have special signals they used with their hunting group. They gathered in groups and cornered even large herbivore reptiles. Their high speed saved them from enemies.

COELOPHYSIS SKELETON

Its skeleton has many bird-like traits: hollow bones, a light body, a tail, and long and thin hind limbs. The coelophysis had short forelimbs with four fingers for grasping. The main body length includes the tail.

The first coelophysis fossils were found by the amateur American palaeontologist David Baldwin in 1881. Baldwin often conducted digs on his own and sent his findings to scientists for further research. In this case, a coelophysis skeleton was first found by Baldwin, but a scientific description was made by the famous palaeontologist Edward Cope.

21

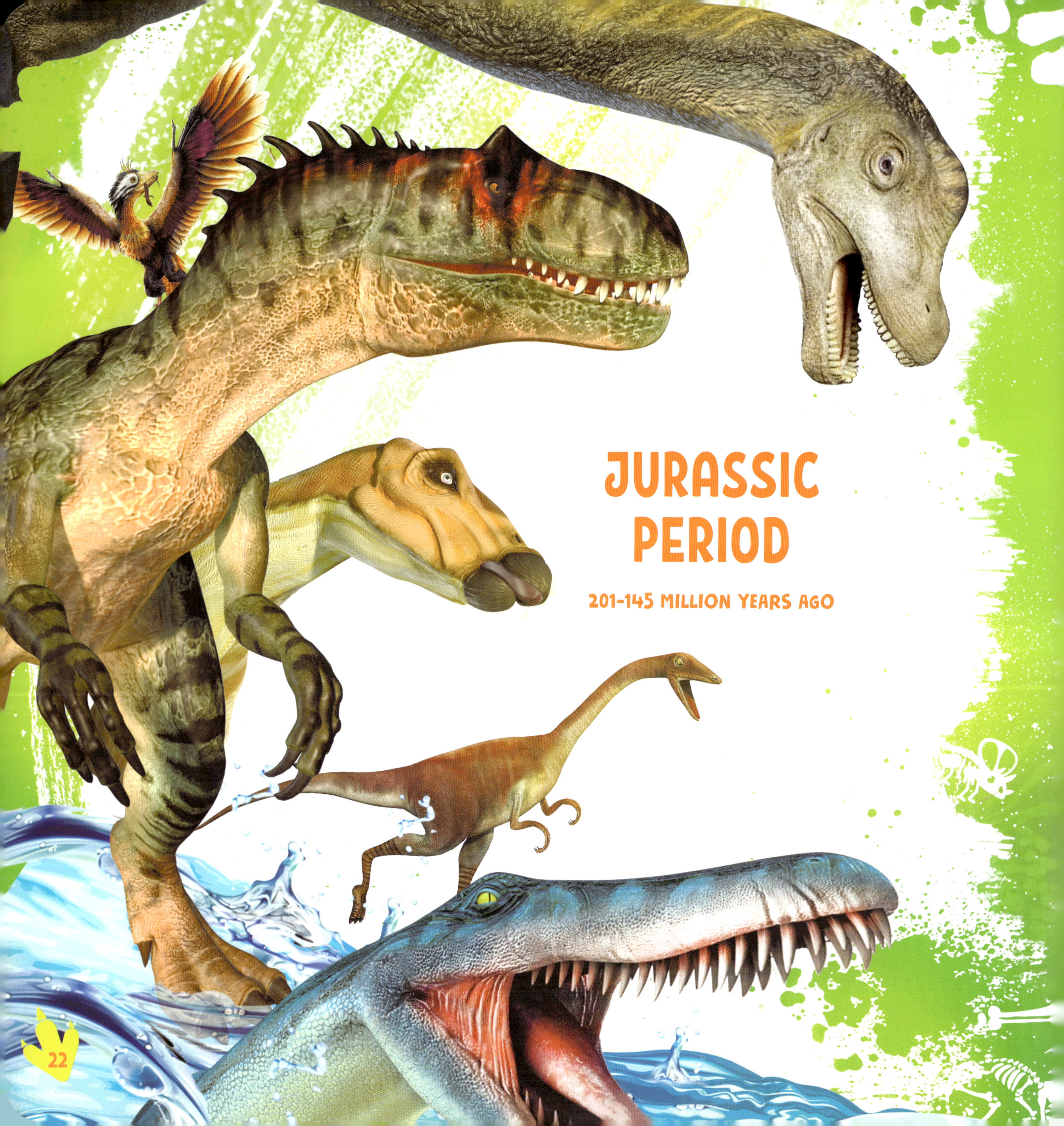

JURASSIC PERIOD
201-145 MILLION YEARS AGO
22

The Jurassic period brought flourishing life everywhere—it was bursting forth from every centimetre, from deep in the ocean to high up in the sky. It was the brightest, most chaotic, and most diverse period of the Mesozoic era. Pangaea was finished splitting into Gondwana and Laurasia, but the continents continued their slow movement, creating new seas and mountain chains. During this period, the first mammals appeared, but dinosaurs remained dominant in the ecosystem.

Volcanic eruptions often made the climate hot and humid. Magma went down the ocean bottom, heating the water and air. This led to heavy rains.

CLIMATE

FAUNA

Many new reptile species formed in this period. They were carnivore and herbivore, small and big, flying and swimming! Also, the first small mammals covered with fur appeared. Molluscs evolved in the seas, as did the first coral reefs, which are very similar to the reefs we have today.

FLORA

The plant community of the Jurassic period was abundant and diverse. Ferns gradually formed vast moorland forests. Sequoias, cypresses, and cycases were gradually replacing grass-like ferns.

Allosauruses usually inhabited dry river valleys that had plenty of water during rainy seasons. Also they chose forests and fern savannahs.

The first allosaurus skeleton was found by palaeontologist Othniel Marsh in 1877. But it only received its dinosaur name in 1970, almost 100 years later! During this gap, scientists found 73 skeletons and got a better idea of this reptile. As a result, they finally managed to give it an appropriate name.

The allosaurus was one of the most dangerous dinosaurs of its time—the king of the Jurassic period! It had sharp claws and deadly jaws, which made it a savage predator!

It had a large skull with eye ridges that could protect its eyes like a visor. It was bipedal, walking on its hind limbs and using its tail for balance.

It could open its jaw almost 90 degrees . . . and that's extremely wide. The bite surface was so large that prey would die of blood loss almost immediately. That's why the allosaurus is considered such an excellent hunter.

The most famous allosaurus skeleton was found in Wyoming, USA, in 1991. It was called Big Al, where "big" means that the skeleton was almost full and well-preserved. Scientists suppose that this skeleton was a teenager and died of an infection. Allosauruses lived up to twenty-five to thirty years and became an adult at fifteen years.

An interesting fact is that allosaurus teeth are the most abundant allosaurus fossils found. Palaeontologists think that their teeth could change and regrew during their whole life. Today allosaurus teeth are sold at auctions all over the world.

BRACHIOSAURUS

152-145 MILLION YEARS AGO

Herbivore

JURASSIC PERIOD

Scientists believe that the brachiosaurus inhabited present-day North America and Africa. During the Jurassic period, there were deserts where drought was replaced by rainy seasons.

Brachiosauruses were so huge that they needed tons of plants to insure enough energy. Their herds were probably constantly migrating in search for food.

The first brachiosaurus fossils were found by palaeontologist Elmer Riggs in 1900, in Colorado, USA. Back then, the brachiosaurus was considered to be a swimming reptile that walked on the ocean floor with its head above water for breathing.

This idea was so interesting that you still can find images by some artists showing brachiosauruses like this, even though this theory was rejected in 1951!

Why couldn't they be water creatures? The water pressure would have made it impossible for brachiosauruses to breathe!

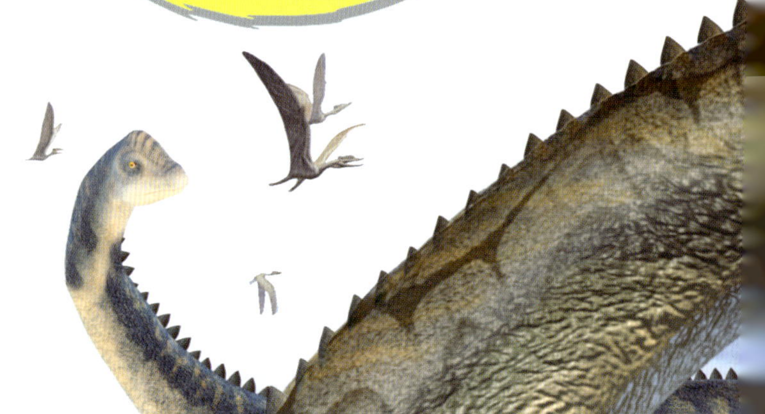

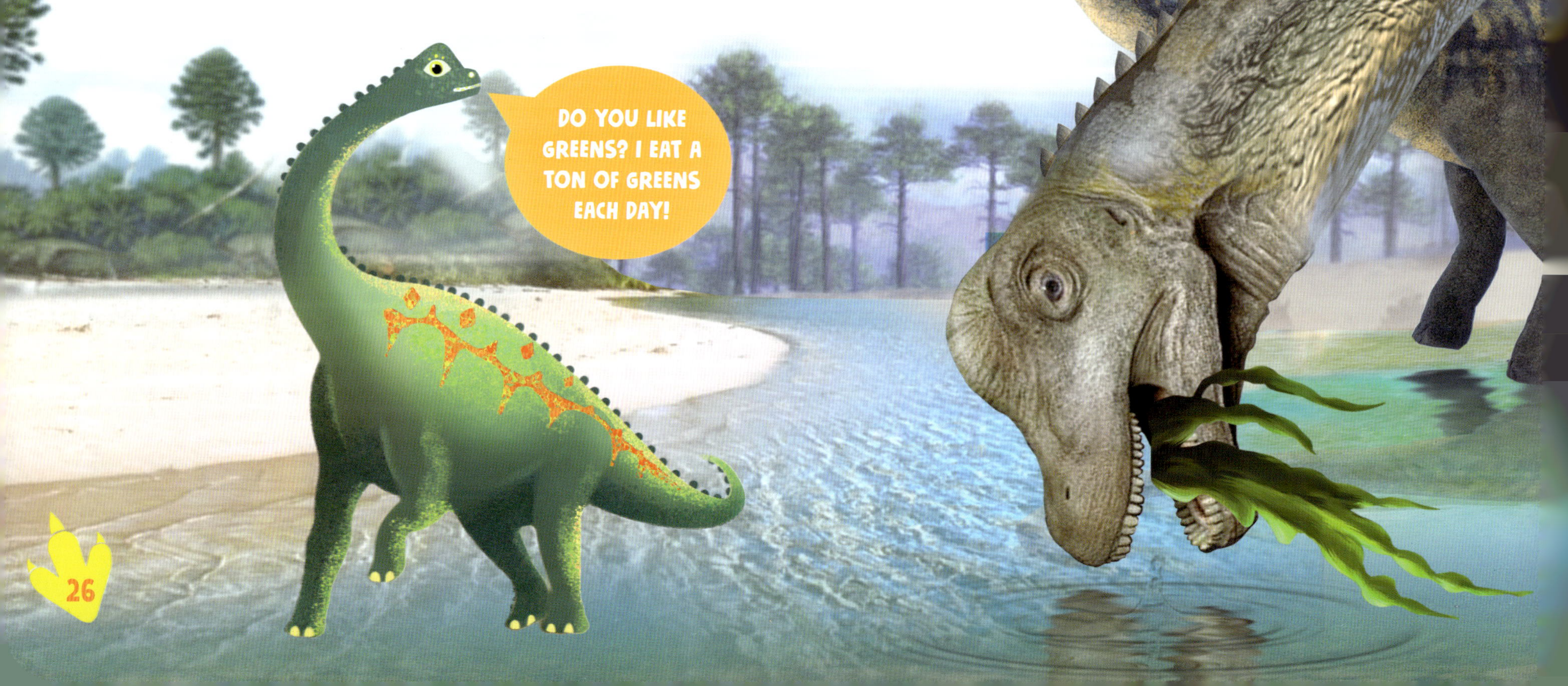

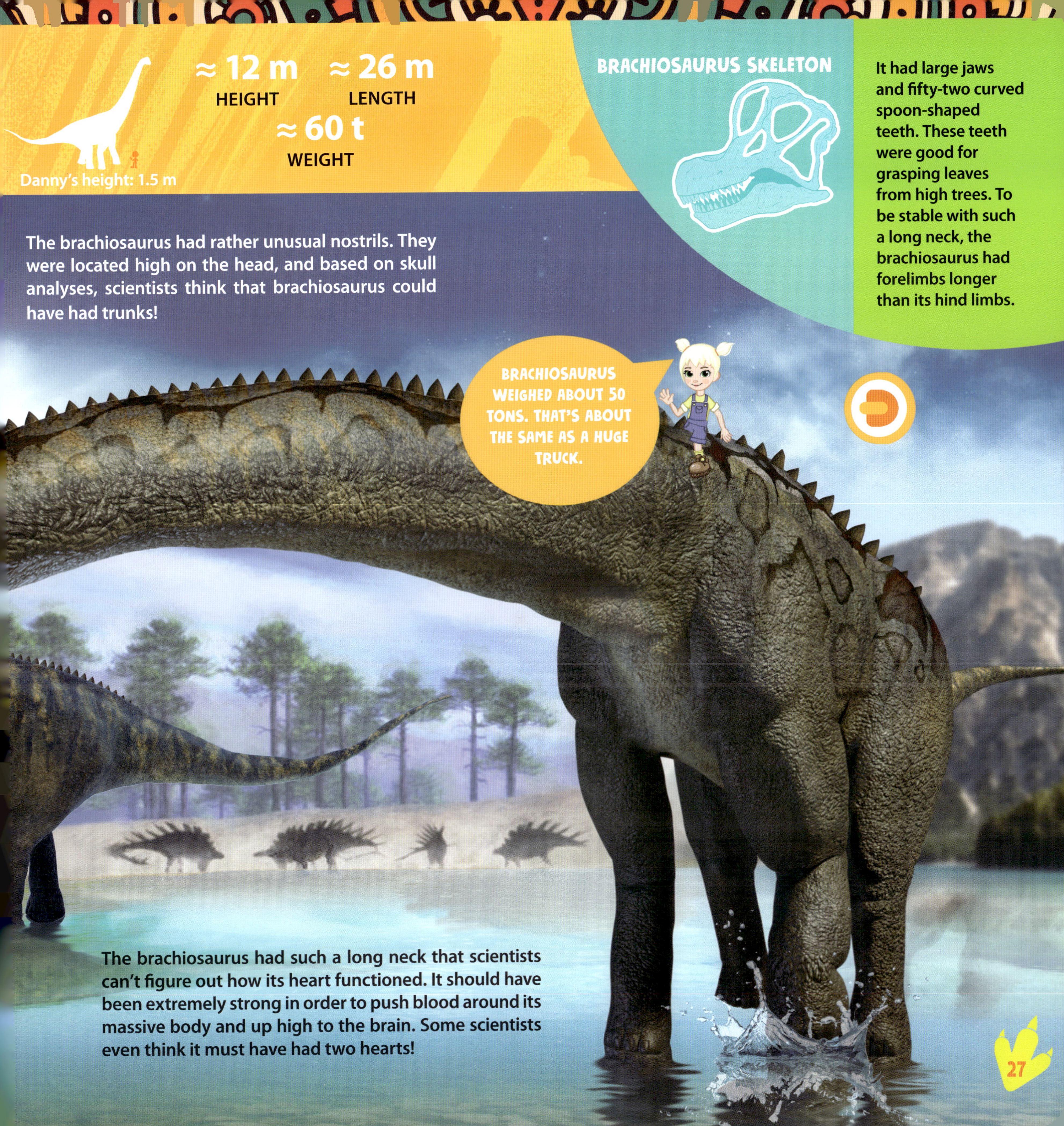

≈ **12 m**
HEIGHT

≈ **26 m**
LENGTH

≈ **60 t**
WEIGHT

Danny's height: 1.5 m

BRACHIOSAURUS SKELETON

It had large jaws and fifty-two curved spoon-shaped teeth. These teeth were good for grasping leaves from high trees. To be stable with such a long neck, the brachiosaurus had forelimbs longer than its hind limbs.

The brachiosaurus had rather unusual nostrils. They were located high on the head, and based on skull analyses, scientists think that brachiosaurus could have had trunks!

The brachiosaurus had such a long neck that scientists can't figure out how its heart functioned. It should have been extremely strong in order to push blood around its massive body and up high to the brain. Some scientists even think it must have had two hearts!

27

STEGOSAURUS

155-145 MILLION YEARS AGO

Herbivore

JURASSIC PERIOD

Stegosauruses lived in dry river valleys that flooded during rainy seasons.

The brain of the stegosaurus was the size of a walnut, so it has a reputation as the most brainless vertebrate.

Palaeontologist Othniel Marsh found the first fossils in 1876. The scientist decided that its plates fastened to its back rather than growing out of it.

The stegosaurus is one of the most recognisable dinosaurs and was even used as a model for Godzilla. This dinosaur was also depicted in *Jurassic Park* and *King Kong*.

It had a small head, spikes on its tail, and seventeen armoured plates on the back. The plates were separate from the internal skeleton, and most likely could move.

Like all lizards with armour, the stegosaurus was rather slow. It is believed that it could go no faster than 5 km/h. Since it couldn't escape from a clever and fast predator, it used its powerful spikes on its tail.

Some scientists say that stegosaurus plates could be not bony, but instead had to be flexible with blood vessels inside. In this case, the plates would have helped the stegosaurus regulate its temperature, but did not perform a protective function, since they could not withstand enemies' blows.

According to another theory, the plates might have been red. This would have helped a stegosaurus not only scare predators but also compete for females.

ARCHAEOPTERYX

150–145 MILLION YEARS AGO

JURASSIC PERIOD

The fossils of the archaeopteryx, the first feathered animal, were found by the German palaeontologist Hermann von Meyer in 1861, in southern Germany.

At this time, the book by Charles Darwin *On the Origin of Species* was actively discussed around the world. And, since the archaeopteryx seemed to combine the features of different animals, it became an excellent example of evolution.

Scientists are still arguing about the avian nature of the archaeopteryx. Could it fly? If so, then how? Did it flap its wings, or did it jump from branch to branch with the air currents? Or maybe it just glided down from great heights?

A developed cerebellum—the part of the brain responsible for whole body movements—indicates that the archaeopteryx could fly. However, its muscles were not sufficiently developed to flap its wings. Most likely, it could take off but only fly a short distance.

≈ **25 cm**
HEIGHT

≈ **0.5 m**
LENGTH

≈ **1 kg**
WEIGHT

Danny's height: 1.5 m

It combines the features of different animals. It had a jaw with teeth, a long tail, a pelvis and ribs, and three fingers with claws . . . just like other dinosaurs. However, its hollow bones, accrete clavicles, and, most importantly, wings and feathers, are characteristic of birds.

In 1861, scientists discovered the fossilised imprint of an unknown animal with plumage. It was a great find since feathers don't usually fossilise. However, this particular archaeopteryx imprint was found in very smooth and soft limestone, which preserved it for millions of years.

One of the first archaeopteryx fossils is kept in the Museum of Natural Science in Berlin. A very funny story is connected with it. They say that it was discovered by a farmer named Jacob Niemeyer, who traded the fossils. . . for a cow! After that, the fossil travelled for a long time, was sold twice, and only after all these adventures, they finally got to the museum.

COMPSOGNATHUS 

150-145 MILLION YEARS AGO

Carnivore

JURASSIC PERIOD

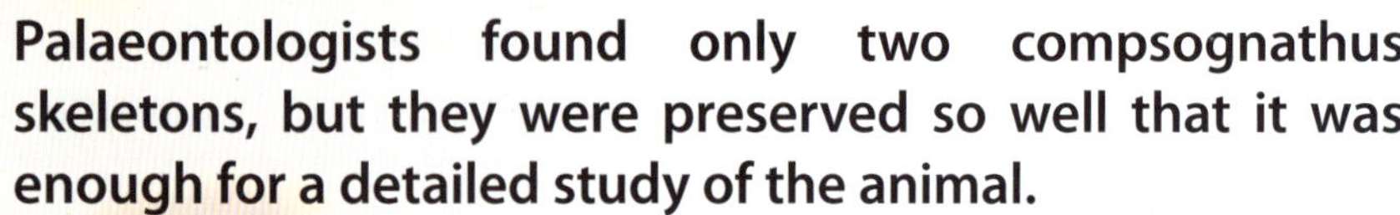

Palaeontologists found only two compsognathus skeletons, but they were preserved so well that it was enough for a detailed study of the animal.

The compsognathus is famous because it dispelled the myth that all dinosaurs were giants. It's hard to believe, but this little guy is about the size of a turkey! Surprisingly, it is not even the smallest, because later, smaller remains were found.

The compsognathus's small, sharp teeth were ideal for hunting. In addition, scientists know what the compsognathus ate. Within one of the fossil remains, scientists found lizard bones!

DINO FACTS

Diet:
insects, lizards, and mammals

Meaning of the name:
"elegant jaw"

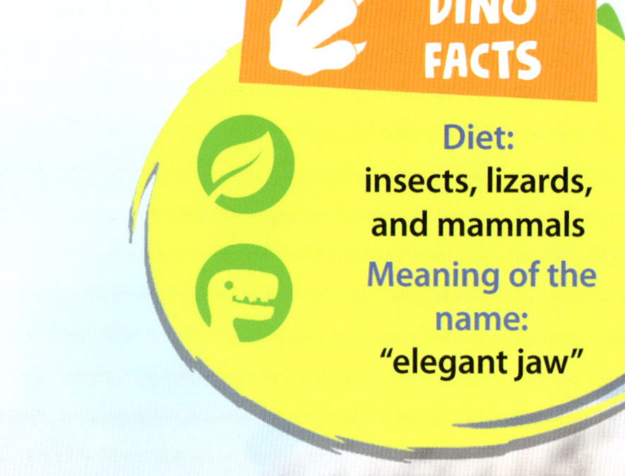

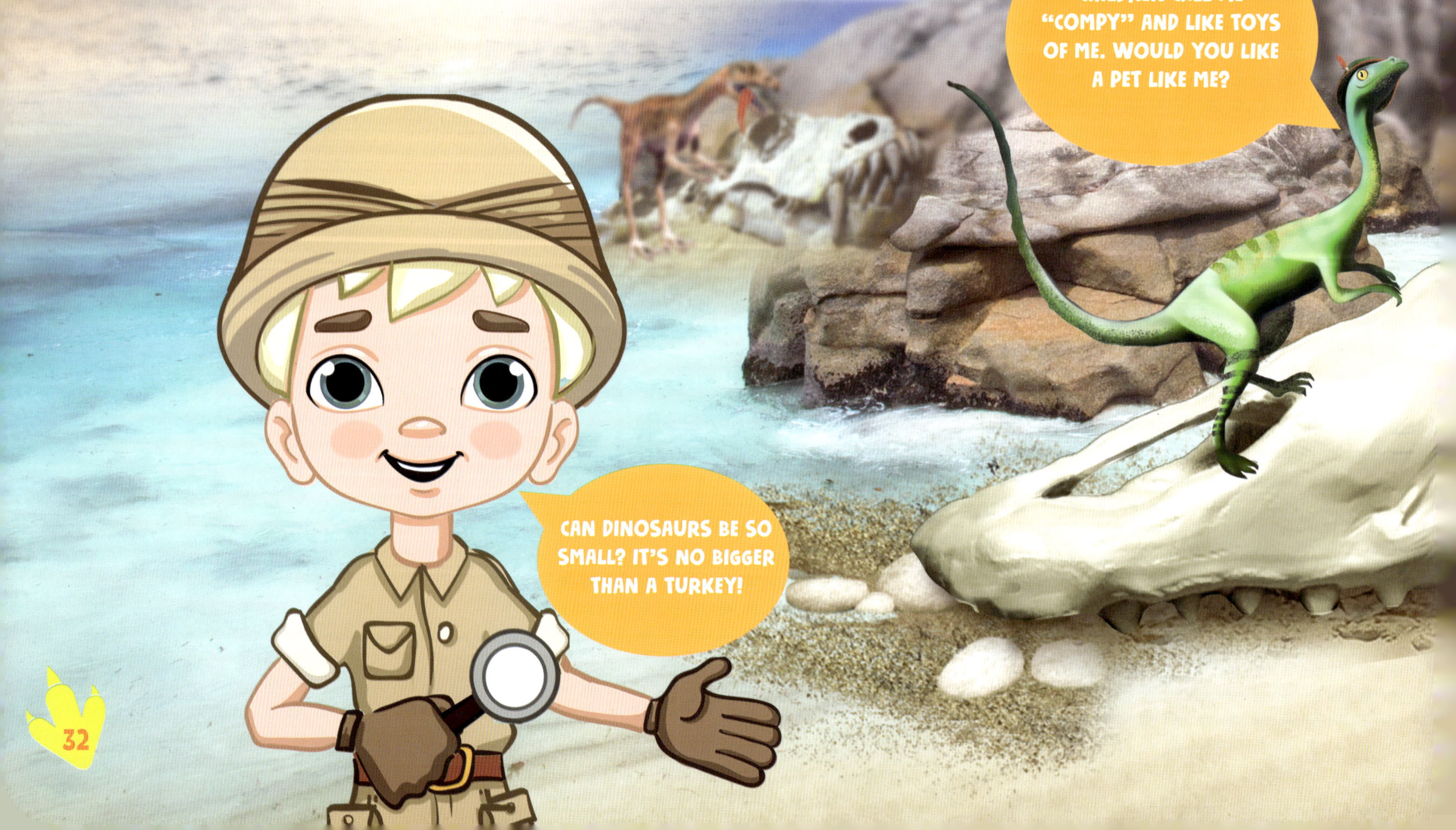

The skeleton structure suggests that the compsognathus was a quick and agile predator. It had a prolonged neck so it could look carefully around, long and thin legs for a quick run, and an elongated tail to keep its balance.

Even though compsognathuses hunted in packs in the movie *Jurassic Park*, they were most likely solitary predators. They probably only occasionally gathered in groups for big hunts.

At first, scientists were convinced that the compsognathus had only two fingers. The third finger "appeared" after a second fossil was found. It became clear then that the first skeleton was not quite complete.

Some believe that the compsognathus was covered with feathers like its close relative the archaeopteryx. However, the remains of compsognathus were without traces of feathering. Who knows, maybe its feathers were very fragile and simply did not survive?

LIOPLEURODON

165–155 MILLION YEARS AGO

Carnivore

JURASSIC PERIOD

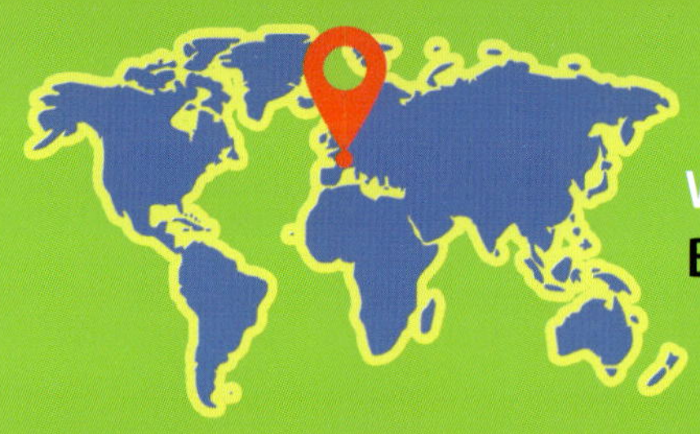

Liopleurodons floated in the seas of the late Jurassic period near modern Europe, mainly in England and France. Most likely, these reptiles could not lay eggs on land and gave birth to ready-for-life cubs. Liopleurodons breathed through their mouths, occasionally rising to the surface.

At first, scientists found only three of liopleurodon teeth. In 1873, the French palaeontologist Henri Emile Sauvage called this lizard "smooth-toothed" and suggested that its length could be 7 meters.

DINO FACTS

Diet:
fish, clams, sea reptiles, and sharks

Meaning of the name:
"smooth-sided tooth"

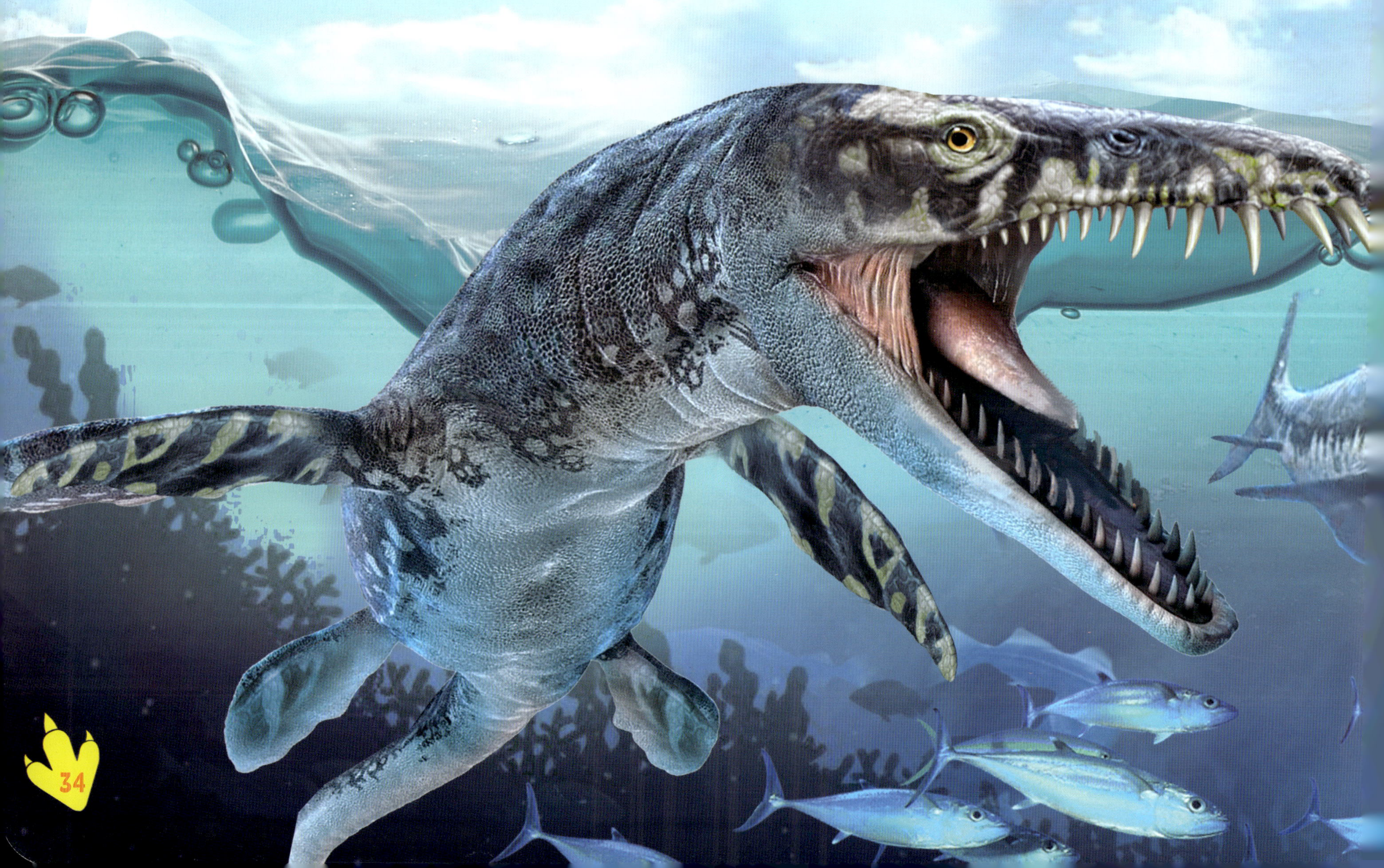

34

≈ 2.5 m
HEIGHT

up to 26 m
LENGTH

up to 45 t
WEIGHT

Danny's height: 1.5 m

LIOPLEURODON SKELETON

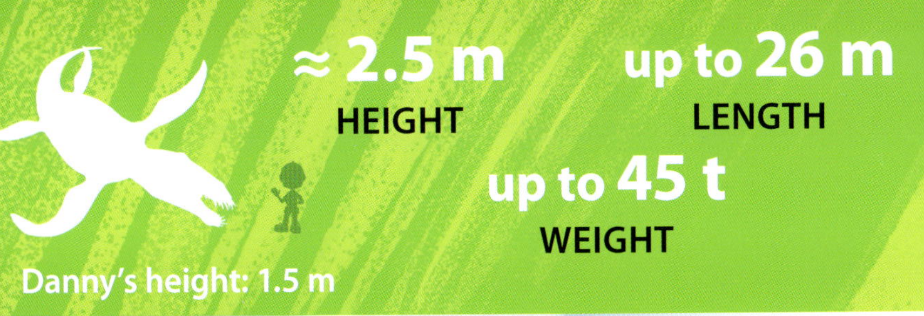

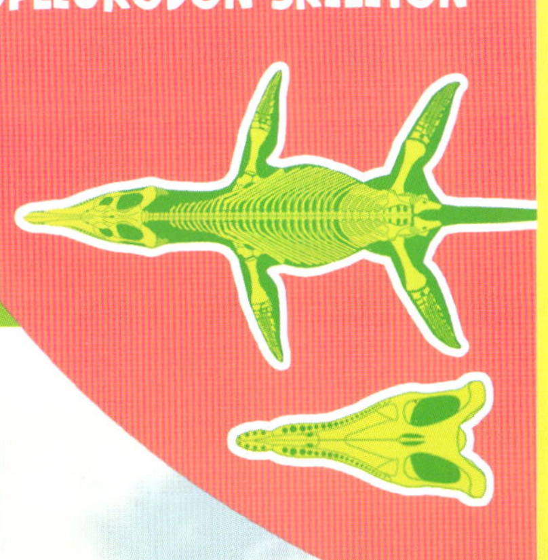

A short tail, narrow head, and powerful flippers provided the liopleurodon with the ability to accelerate rapidly underwater.
It could manoeuvre perfectly and move quickly through the water.

In the 1999 BBC television series *Walking with Dinosaurs*, the liopleurodon was shown as a 26-meter predator weighing 150 tons. This is most likely an exaggeration, but scientists are sure that it was the largest marine predator with almost no enemies.

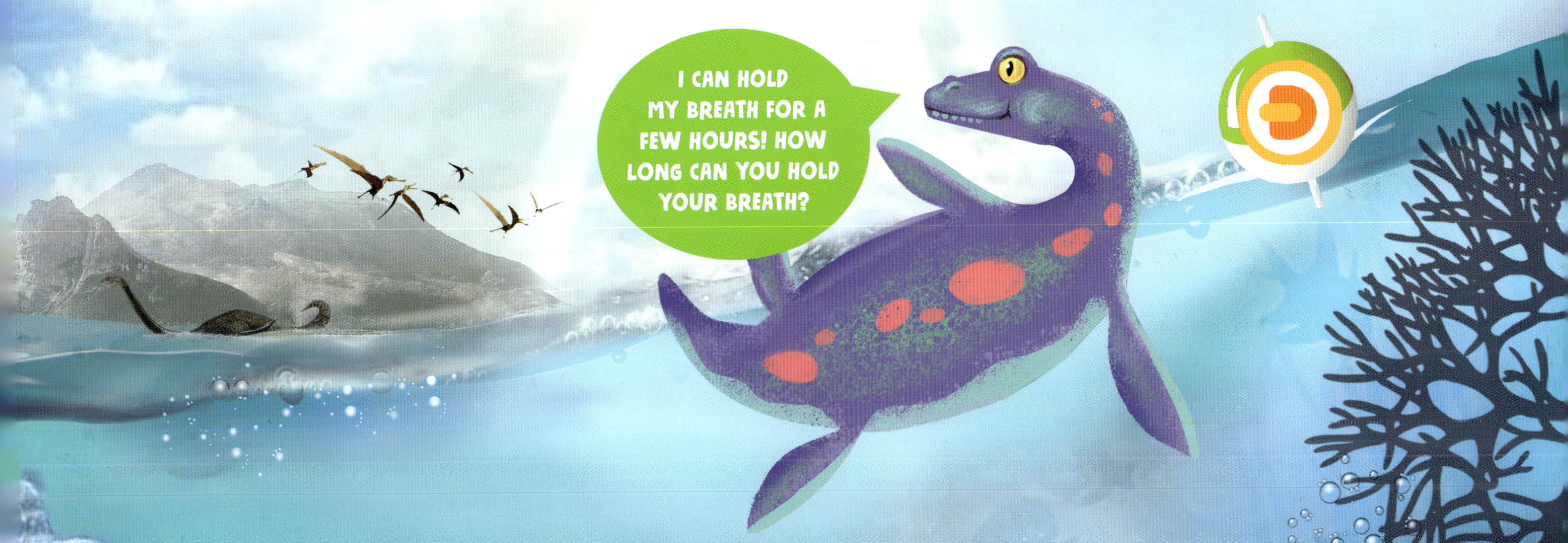

Palaeontologists agree that the liopleurodon was very fast, but only over short distances. It could suddenly pounce on prey from a hiding place.

Skull examinations show that the liopleurodon had a unique nose. It "sniffed" the water in search of prey, passing it through the internal and external nostrils. This gave it the ability to smell the victim even at great distances. It spent hours waiting for prey in ambush, holding its breath for hours at a time.

Disputes over its size are still ongoing because palaeontologists have only found this creature's skull and teeth so far.

CRETACEOUS
PERIOD
145-66 MILLION YEARS AGO
36

During the Cretaceous period, the most famous dinosaur species, including iguanodons, triceratops, and, of course, the famous tyrannosaurus rex, appeared. Laurasia and Gondwana continued breaking apart. Africa, India, and Australia began to move away from each other. Giant islands formed, and the Atlantic Ocean broadened.

Around 120 million years ago, a global cooling began that lasted more than a million years. Then, volcanoes in the Indian Ocean erupted, and the climate became hot again. Still, after half a century from the warming, the Earth began to cool again. According to one version of events, the oceans could not absorb all the heat and reflected it into the atmosphere. At the end of the Cretaceous period, the climate warmed again.

CLIMATE

FAUNA

Bees and butterflies evolved. Mammals were still small and looked like mice. The largest winged creatures in history, such as quetzalcoatlus, soared in the sky, but numerous bird species were gradually displacing them. Thus, flying lizards and birds existed at that time.

FLORA

During the Cretaceous period, the first flowers appeared. They were pollinated by numerous insects. Thanks to insects, flowering plants spread rapidly throughout the world. Their roots prevented the soil from erosion. This meant that fewer minerals fell into the seas, and underwater plants became scarcer.

Triceratopses lived in the forests and marshes of North America. Scientists believe that their main food were plants that were close to the ground, because of the low placement of their head.

Triceratops moved on four paws that were as thick as pillars. The front paws were more powerful than the hind ones, since they held the massive head and collar bone.

In 1887, John Bell Hatcher found horns with skull fragments in Colorado, USA. Even the most experienced palaeontologists suggested that they belonged to a prehistoric buffalo. However, two years later, they found another skull, and then no one had any doubts it was a dinosaur.

In 1994, the most complete triceratops skeleton, nicknamed Raymond, was discovered. It is one of the most complete specimens ever, and it helped prove that triceratops had massive legs.

Triceratops existed until the end of the Mesozoic era. They were one of the last dinosaurs on Earth.

3 m
HEIGHT
9 m
LENGTH
9 t
WEIGHT
Danny's height: 1.5 m

TRICERATOPS SKELETON

Its skull is the most recognisable features of this dinosaur.
The skull is 2 meters in length, has three horns, and a bone "collar."

A triceratops's life was full of adventures and dangers, as it lived at the same time as the T-rex, the most formidable predator of the Cretaceous period. On one triceratops skull, scientists found T-rex bite marks. This suggests that dinosaurs met in everyday life, and such meetings were not very friendly.

IT'S SUCH A BEAST!
LIKE A RHINO WITH A
PARROT BEAK!

39

SPINOSAURUS

70–66 MILLION YEARS AGO

Carnivore

CRETACEOUS PERIOD

The spinosaurus inhabited river basins of the modern territories of North Africa.

Most scientists agree that spinosaurus's main diet was fish. It had narrow long jaws with big sharp teeth—ideal for grasping slippery prey like frogs or fish. The spinosaurus was probably one of the largest and most dangerous predators of its time.

For about 100 years, the idea of spinosaurus's appearance was constantly changing. The reason is that we lack a complete skeleton, so scientists can only guess. They don't even know if it walked on two or four legs!

DINO FACTS

Diet:
fish and water reptiles

Meaning of the name:
"spine lizard"

When first discovered, scientists couldn't understand how some of its features worked. The theory that this was a water dweller solved most of the mysteries!

The spinosaurus could be the only actual dinosaur that could swim. But this theory is still debated.

It's still unknown why the spinosaurus needed a sail. One theory states that it raised the sail to frighten enemies. Another theory says that the sail was used to regulate its temperature. It could also be used as a fin during underwater fishing.

If the spinosaurus was a land animal, it wouldn't have been able to run very fast. It would have attacked prey by lying in wait and then ambushing its meal. The dinosaur was big, and the sail was not good for camouflage.

ANKYLOSAURUS

74-66 MILLION YEARS AGO

Herbivore

CRETACEOUS PERIOD

Ankylosauruses lived in the same forests as triceratops and tyrannosauruses. They were very slow plant-eating animals with very short and massive legs.

The most unique feature of the ankylosaurus was its armour. Its whole body, except the stomach, was covered with thick, bony plates. Even its eyes had armour!

The tail ended in a large club. It was heavy enough to break predators' legs.

On the both sides of its head there were four horns, so it was impossible to bite this dinosaur's neck. And to protect its soft belly, it could dig itself in the ground, so the predator had to deal with its armour.

The ankylosaurus had a weak jaw and small teeth. It was more likely to swallow food than chew it. For sure it had big organs and a good appetite!

Danny's height: 1.5 m
1.7 m
HEIGHT
9 m
LENGTH
≈ 6 t
WEIGHT
ANKYLOSAURUS SKELETON
It got its name "spine lizard" because of its bent back bones. The body was covered with shell and spines, with a tail that ended with a bony club. This was its defence armour.
Some researchers believe that the ankylosaurus's armour was not hard but was instead used to attract females.
The nose was rather sensitive and could pick up a predator's scent from a long distance away. The dinosaur could eat and breathe at the same time, just like humans, but unlike most other reptiles.
The ankylosaurus used its nose for thermoregulation: breathing out hot air and inhaling cool air. Dogs use their tongues the same way.
43

ELASMOSAURUS

85-66 MILLION YEARS AGO

CRETACEOUS PERIOD

The elasmosaurus was not quite a dinosaur. To be precise, it wasn't a dinosaur at all. It was a swimming reptile, called a plesiosaurus. Scientists believe they couldn't lay eggs on land, so they gave birth to live youth in the water.

It's highly likely that they couldn't breathe underwater, so they had to rise up every 10 to 20 minutes to breathe.

Some palaeontologists believe that the Loch Ness Monster, Nessie, is an elasmosaurus! Is it possible that one dinosaur survived extinction?

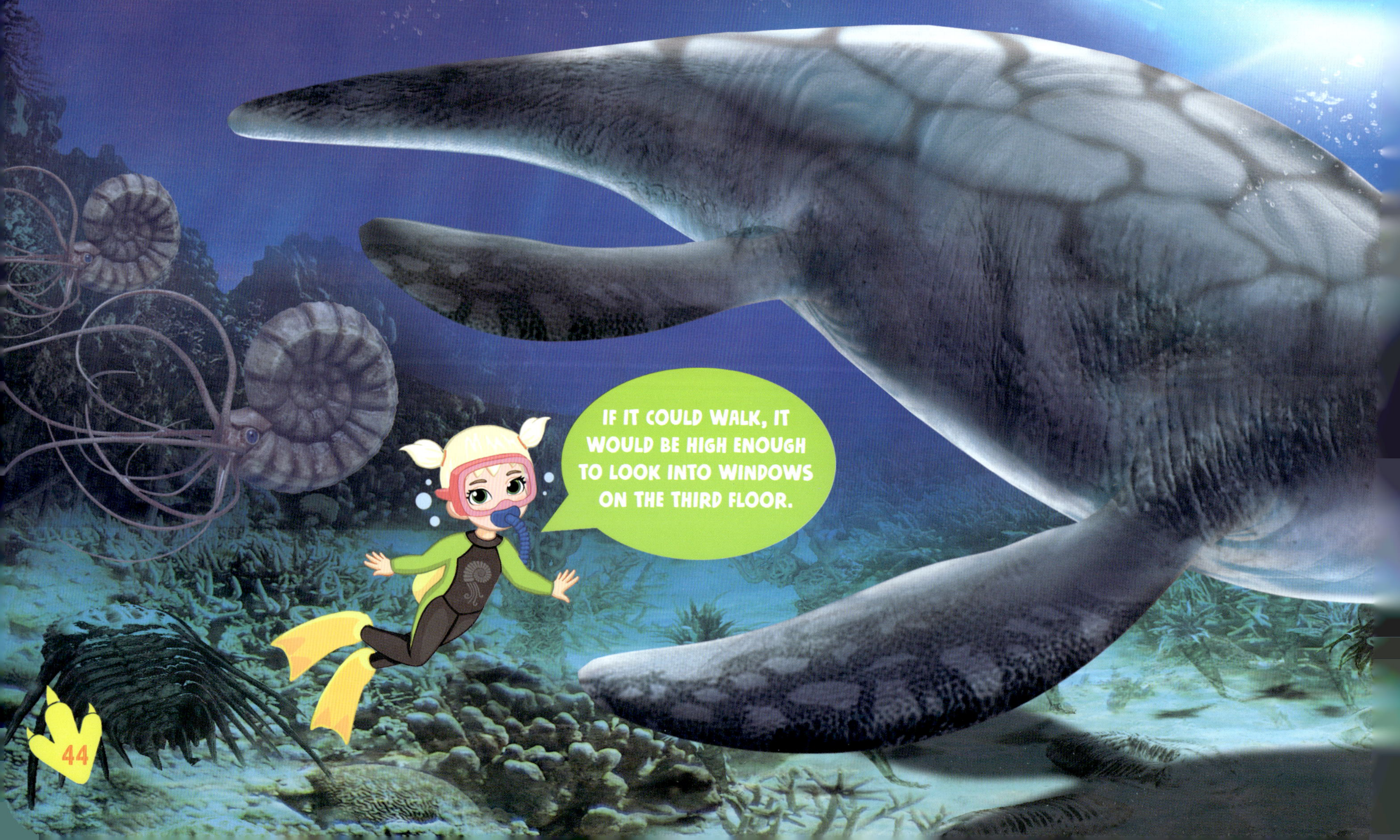

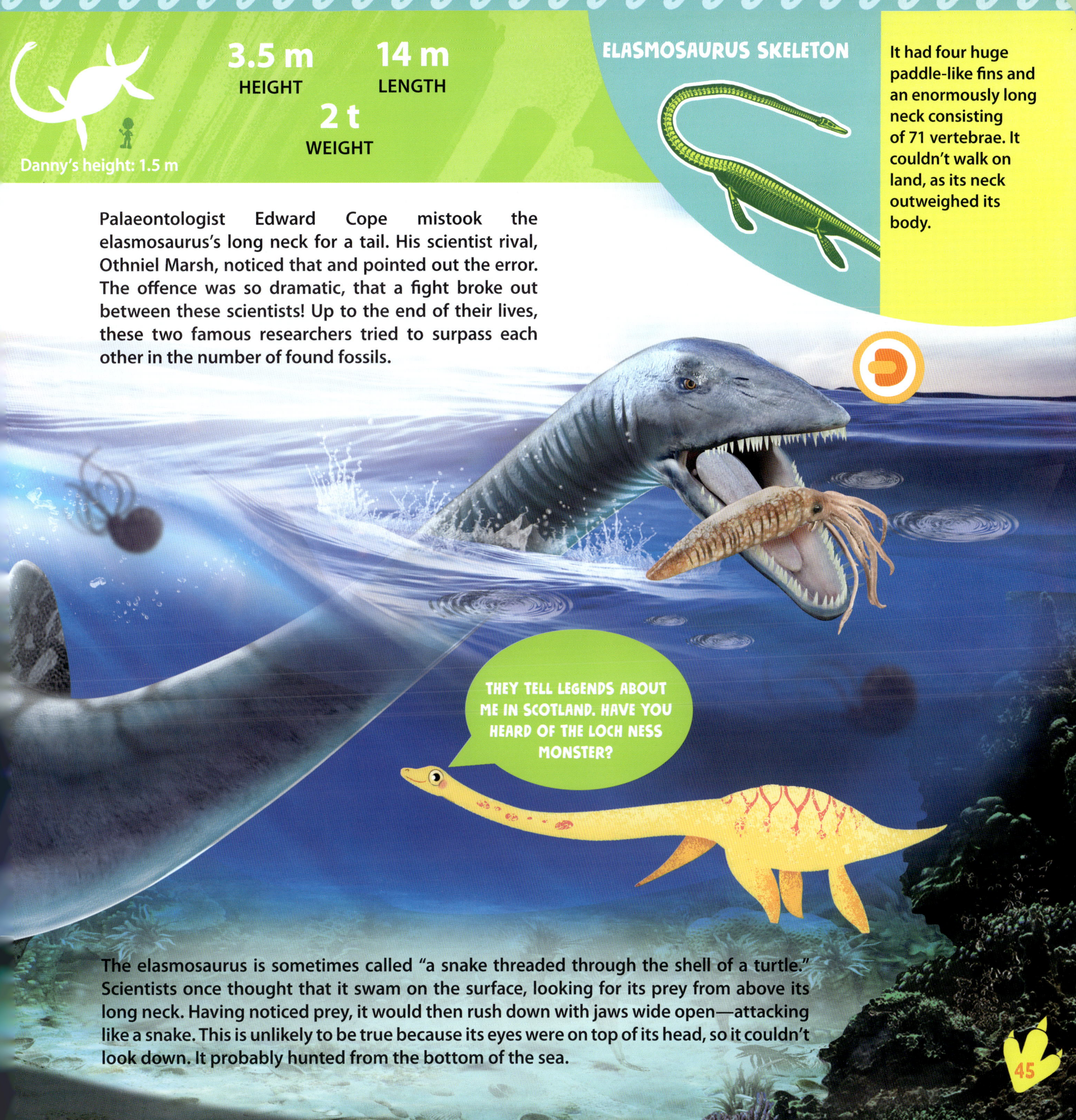

It had four huge paddle-like fins and an enormously long neck consisting of 71 vertebrae. It couldn't walk on land, as its neck outweighed its body.

Palaeontologist Edward Cope mistook the elasmosaurus's long neck for a tail. His scientist rival, Othniel Marsh, noticed that and pointed out the error. The offence was so dramatic, that a fight broke out between these scientists! Up to the end of their lives, these two famous researchers tried to surpass each other in the number of found fossils.

The elasmosaurus is sometimes called "a snake threaded through the shell of a turtle." Scientists once thought that it swam on the surface, looking for its prey from above its long neck. Having noticed prey, it would then rush down with jaws wide open—attacking like a snake. This is unlikely to be true because its eyes were on top of its head, so it couldn't look down. It probably hunted from the bottom of the sea.

QUETZALCOATLUS

69-66 MILLION YEARS AGO

Carnivore

CRETACEOUS PERIOD

This lizard got its name from the ancient Aztec deity—the feathered, winged serpent Quetzalcoatl, the god of rain and wind. Unlike it, the lizard's body wasn't covered with feathers but with pycnofibers, which are special body covers like human hair or animal fur.

Part of a quetzalcoatlus's wing was discovered by palaeontologist Douglas Lawson in 1971 in Big Bend National Park (Texas, USA). The scientist suggested that the lizard could belong to pterosaurs.

DINO FACTS

Diet:
fish, crabs, worms

Meaning of the name:
"feathered serpent"

46

≈ **6 m**
HEIGHT

up to **11 m**
LENGTH

up to **250 kg**
WEIGHT

QUETZALCOATLUS SKELETON

It had light, hollow bones, a straight, long beak with no teeth, and small eyes. Though scientists failed to find a complete skeleton, they suggest that it had a very long neck.

Quetzalcoatlus might be the largest flying creature on the planet, but scientists still argue about whether this lizard could actually fly.

Judging by its skeleton, it was very large. With such dimensions, it probably couldn't fly high in the sky. That is why some believe that the quetzalcoatlus used its wings to accelerate on the ground and then glided in the air.

Quetzalcoatlus most likely had a long, thin neck, short hind legs, and bulky forelimbs. It could lean on them to walk on all fours, and most likely looked very awkward doing so. Perhaps it looked like a modern giraffe. They are about the same height!

TYRANNOSAURUS

68-66 MILLION YEARS AGO

Carnivore

CRETACEOUS PERIOD

Where was it found?
Montana, USA

Tyrannosaurus rex, often called T. rex, was one of the most dangerous and fierce predators on the planet! Some people believe that it loved hunting triceratops.

The hind limbs of a tyrannosaurus were heavy and strong, while its forelimbs were small. Its hind limbs made this dinosaur the most dangerous predator. It felt every single vibration of the ground and could easily detect another dinosaur nearby.

DINO FACTS

Diet:
other dinosaurs

Meaning of the name:
"tyrant lizard"

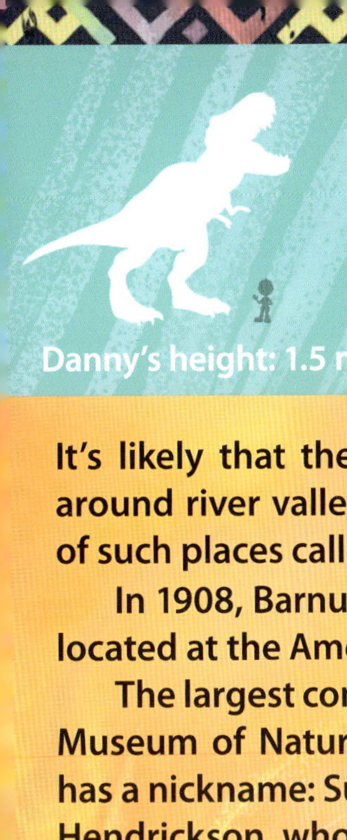

SKELETON OF TYRANNOSAURUS

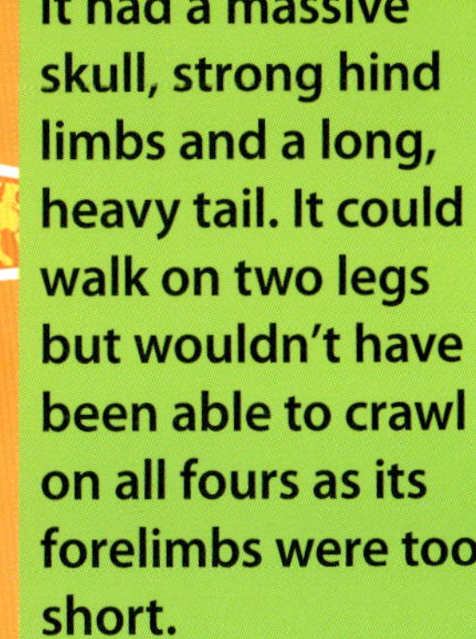

It had a massive skull, strong hind limbs and a long, heavy tail. It could walk on two legs but wouldn't have been able to crawl on all fours as its forelimbs were too short.

It's likely that the tyrannosaurus inhabited forests and around river valleys. Its first fossils were found near one of such places called Hell Creek (Montana, USA).

In 1908, Barnum Brown discovered a full fossilised skeleton. Today it is located at the American Museum of Natural History in New York.

The largest complete skeleton of a tyrannosaurus is located at the Field Museum of Natural History in Chicago. As all other famous skeletons, it has a nickname: Sue. It was named after the famous palaeontologist Susan Hendrickson, who discovered it in 1997.

It is believed that T-rex is one of the most known and well-studied dinosaurs. It has become a character in many movies, books, and even video games!

As of now, more than 50 perfect skeletons of tyrannosauruses have been found!

A very long time ago, dinosaurs reigned on our planet, dominating on land, in water, and in the sky. But approximately 65 million years ago, they all disappeared. There are many theories as to how and why the dinosaurs went extinct; however scientists continue to debate this issue. According to the most recent research studies, at the end of the Cretaceous period dinosaurs were already on the verge of extinction. It was hard for them to adapt to the changing climate. And indeed, new species such as birds and mammals started dynamically inhabiting our planet. So the meteoritic impact simply rushed things along.

THE MOST POPULAR THEORY

METEORITIC FALL

According to the most popular belief, the reason of the "great extinction" of the dinosaurs was a meteoritic fall in the area of the Mexican peninsula, Yucatan. As a result of this collision so much dense cloud arose that the Sun was eclipsed for very long time. Plants stopped growing, and the dinosaurs died of starvation.

DO YOU KNOW WHAT A METEORITE IS?
THEY ARE STONE OR IRON SPACE DEBRIS, WHICH RUN INTO THE ATMOSPHERE OF THE EARTH. THEY CAN BE REALLY SMALL (NOT BIGGER THAN A GRAM) OR GIANT (SEVERAL DOZENS OF TONES). IN MOST CASES, METEORITES BURN UP IN THE ATMOSPHERE, BUT SOMETIMES, VERY RARELY, THEY MANAGE TO REACH THE SURFACE OF THE EARTH.

RAVENOUS INSECTS

There is another theory that the extinction of dinosaurs was caused by … butterflies! Their ravenous caterpillars destroyed all the plants around, and in that manner, they deprived herbivorous dinosaurs of food. Predatory lizards were also starving, so they went extinct as well. Some of the birds and insectivorous mammals, who are the successors of dinosaurs, survived.

CARNIVORES

Some scientists believe that dinosaurs could have been hunted to extinction by the first carnivorous mammals. They fed on helpless babies and destroyed clutches of eggs.

VOLCANIC ERUPTIONS

Many scientists think that dinosaurs' extinction could have been caused by endless volcanic eruptions. Frequent ashfalls and carbon dioxide emissions could have changed the atmosphere composition, making the air unbreathable and causing a global freezing.

CLIMATIC CHANGES

Danger could have come from sharp climate changes that happened back at the time. The split of continents caused volcanic eruptions and new rock formations. The composition and level of the global sea was constantly changing, and the temperature was bouncing from freezing cold to unbearable heat.

In spite of wide variety of different theories, the true cause of the extinction of the dinosaurs remains a mystery.
WHAT DO YOU THINK HAPPENED?

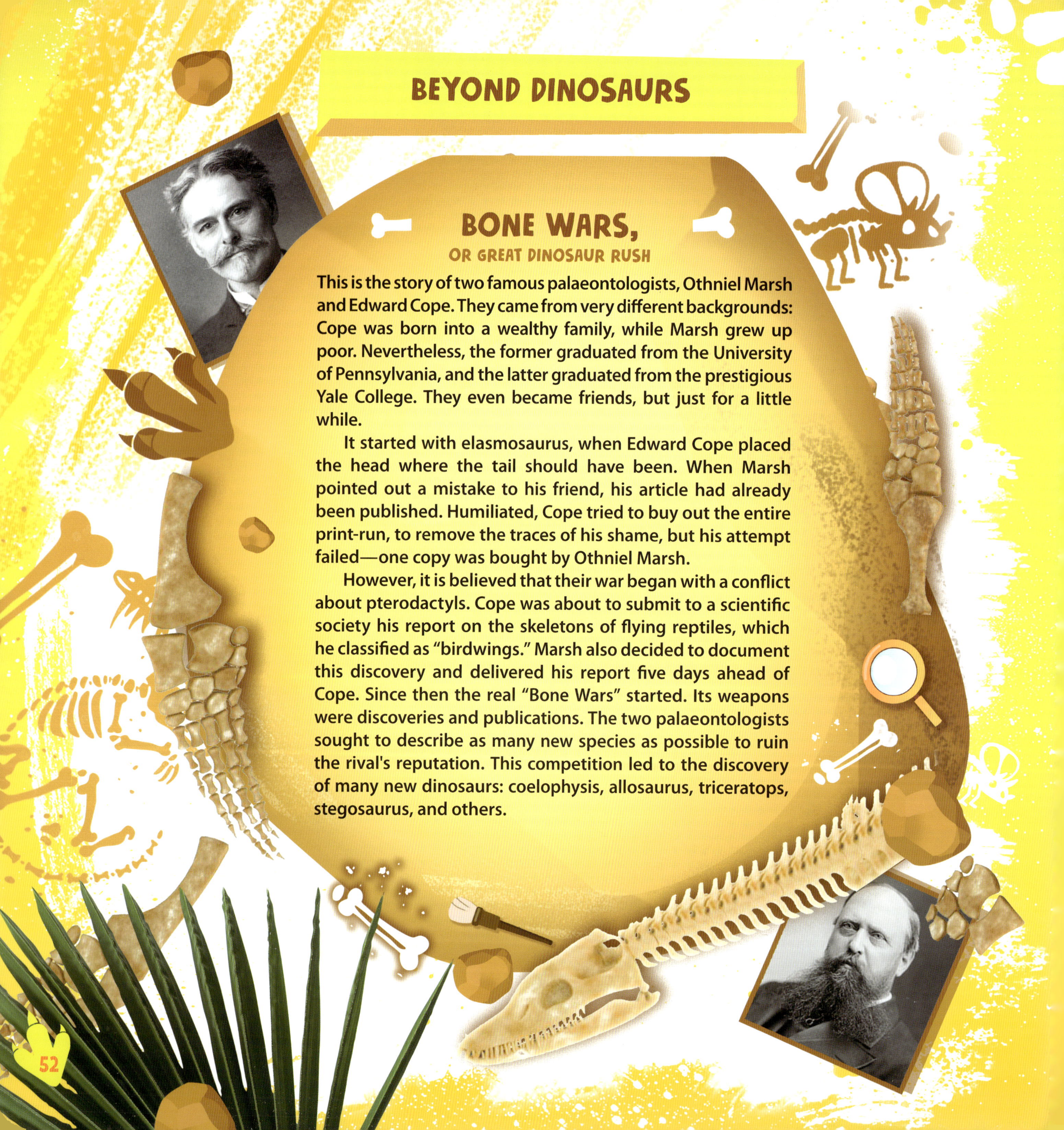

BONE WARS,
OR GREAT DINOSAUR RUSH

This is the story of two famous palaeontologists, Othniel Marsh and Edward Cope. They came from very different backgrounds: Cope was born into a wealthy family, while Marsh grew up poor. Nevertheless, the former graduated from the University of Pennsylvania, and the latter graduated from the prestigious Yale College. They even became friends, but just for a little while.

It started with elasmosaurus, when Edward Cope placed the head where the tail should have been. When Marsh pointed out a mistake to his friend, his article had already been published. Humiliated, Cope tried to buy out the entire print-run, to remove the traces of his shame, but his attempt failed—one copy was bought by Othniel Marsh.

However, it is believed that their war began with a conflict about pterodactyls. Cope was about to submit to a scientific society his report on the skeletons of flying reptiles, which he classified as "birdwings." Marsh also decided to document this discovery and delivered his report five days ahead of Cope. Since then the real "Bone Wars" started. Its weapons were discoveries and publications. The two palaeontologists sought to describe as many new species as possible to ruin the rival's reputation. This competition led to the discovery of many new dinosaurs: coelophysis, allosaurus, triceratops, stegosaurus, and others.

SUSAN HENDRICKSON

The life of Susan Hendrickson is by no means boring! She managed to try her hand at the most extraordinary occupations: she hunted tropical fish and mined amber in the Dominican Republic. During her research, Susan discovered three perfect 23-million-year-old butterflies. She also unearthed the largest T-rex skeleton, which was nicknamed Sue in her honour.

ARCHOSAURS

A group of ancient reptiles whose living representatives consist of crocodiles, birds, and dinosaurs.

DINOSAURS

A group of ancient reptiles that lived only on land.

LAVA

Or magma, is molten rock produced by a volcano.

CYCASES

Tall, palm tree-shaped plants (up to 15 meters tall).

MAMMALS

Animals that feed their babies with milk. Mammals appeared on Earth at the end of the Triassic period around the same time as dinosaurs.

HERBIVORES

Animals that eat only plant food.

GINKGOS

Short trees with long, fan-shaped leaves.

PLESIOSAURIA

A group of ancient reptiles that had long necks and lived in the sea.

PTEROSAURIA

A group of flying reptiles whose wings were covered with skin stretched between body and the fourth finger of the forelimb.

REPTILES

Or reptilians, are ectothermic vertebrates. Their skin is covered in scales and they lay eggs on land.

SUPERCONTINENT

A single large landmass, which existed long ago. It was named Pangaea.

CARNIVORES

Animals that hunt other animals and live on meat.

BARNUM BROWN

Barnum Brown is best known as one of the most famous fossil hunters of the 20th century. During his investigations, the palaeontologist traversed the country searching for fossils. He discovered the first remains of tyrannosaurus rex and brought more than 300 large artefacts from the expedition. Brown preferred field studies and was less concerned with publishing his discoveries. Enthusiastic followers even named him Mr. Bones.

Content and colours may vary.

WOW!

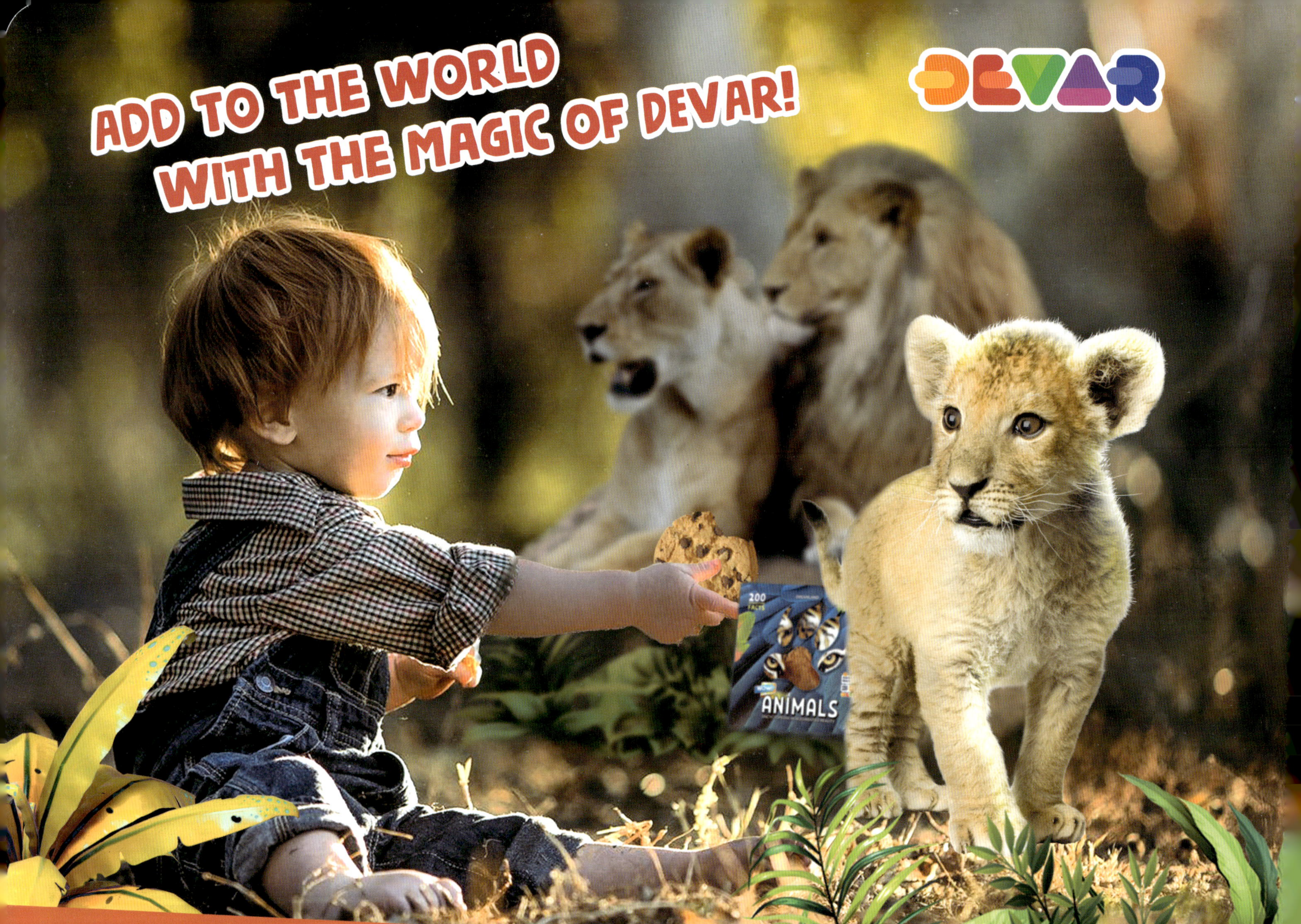

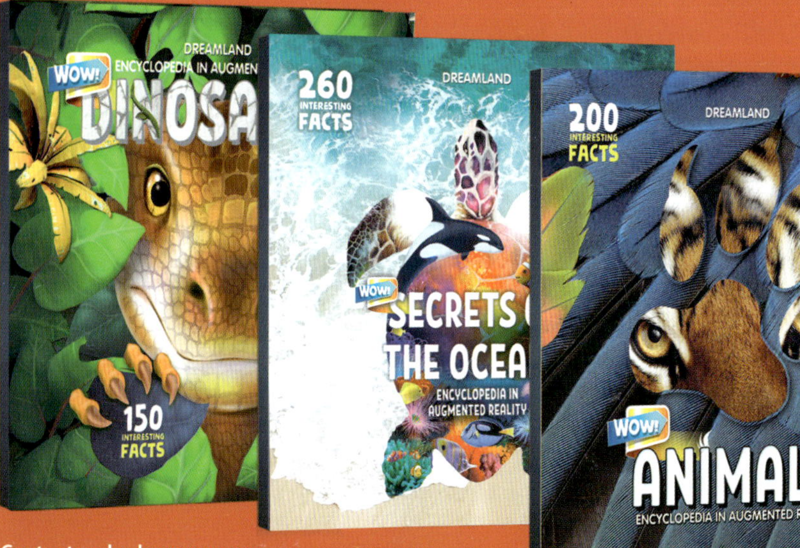

ENCYCLOPEDIAS

Go on an amazing adventure with the miraculous DEVAR encyclopedias! Look into the remotest places of the universe, uncover many mysteries and even travel through time!

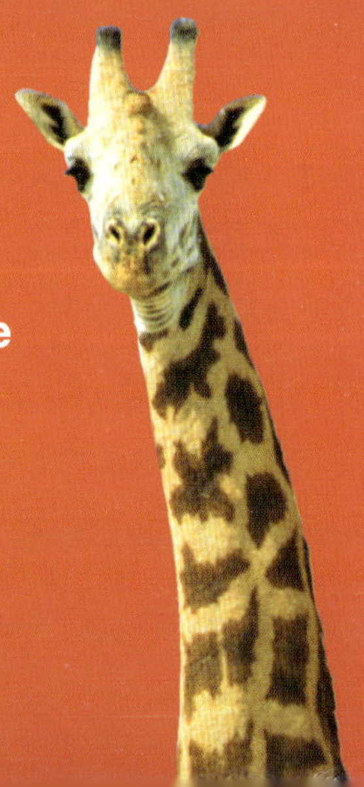